The 5 Stages of Grief

A comprehensive and insightful guide to the grief and loss process. Learn a clear and concise explanation of the five stages of grief, as well as helpful tips for coping with loss. Understand what you may be feeling and going through and learn to move on healthily.

4

6

Introduction

The death of someone close to us often creates a complex set of emotions. We often experience a range of different feelings over a week or two after death, each stage lasting for a further period. The grief cycle is based on five stages, and it's normal for each of us to experience them at different times, depending on our age, personality, family situation, and experience. There's no right or wrong way to experience grief, but it's essential to understand the stages to help yourself through them.

In order to deal with the death of someone close to you, you first have to understand how the grieving process works. Death is always a sad event. Everyone reacts differently to death, and that is because everyone has their unique ways of dealing with it. The most important thing to remember about death is that nothing lasts forever.

Grief is an emotional response to the loss of someone close to us. There are five stages to the grief cycle. Each of them lasts for a specific amount of time. In addition, there is also an intensity factor. Some grief stages feel more potent than others, and some people may experience more intense grief. If you are feeling overwhelmed, remember that you're not alone. Other people think the same way. Feelings may change from day to day, so don't worry if you feel one way today and another way tomorrow.

The most important thing to know is that people experience grief differently. Some people go through the five stages of grief almost immediately. In contrast, others take weeks or months to share the first stage. Everyone has their own personal pace, but it's not uncommon to feel different emotions during the five stages.

It's normal for anyone to experience grief and sorrow after the loss of someone special in their life. It's a universal emotion that has been around since the beginning of civilization. It usually lasts for one to three years, but it varies from person to person. Some people never completely recover from a loss, while others learn to live with it. For some people, grief is more complicated than for others. For example, some people may feel guilty about a loss because they feel like they didn't do enough to prevent it. Some people even blame themselves for death. On the other hand, others might have to deal with the emotional pain for a long time, even though they are healthy and physically fit.

There are some people who have a more challenging time dealing with loss. These people are usually compassionate. They can be easily hurt or upset. They have low self-esteem and may believe that they are not good enough to survive independently. They may think about the person they lost and wish they could get back together again.

It's also important to realize that sometimes the grieving process goes on for a long time. A person may grieve the loss of someone who has passed away for months or even years. Sometimes, the death of a loved one is very traumatic, and people cannot deal with it properly.

You should try to understand the stages of grief. It can help you understand the feelings of other people better. It can also help you deal with your grief. You can do this by talking to friends and family members. You can also speak to counselors and psychologists. It's also essential to make sure that you are eating and getting plenty of rest.

The 5 Stages of Grief book will help you through your grief. It will help you understand where the grief comes from, the stages, and how you can deal with it.

The first thing you need to do is understand that grief is natural. People often experience sadness after losing a loved one or an object. They may also grieve when they are disappointed. They may grieve when they lose their job, when they are diagnosed with a severe illness, and when they lose their home. Some people may even suffer when they lose their beloved pet. There is nothing wrong with experiencing grief. However, people sometimes think that if they feel sad or sad about something, they are not strong enough or weak.

But they are not. Grief is a normal human emotion, and you should not feel bad about experiencing it. People who don't experience grief are called non-criers. It is essential to understand that there is no shame or blame when you experience grief. Feelings of sorrow are natural and healthy emotions. People who are strong and confident will be able to handle the negative emotions associated with grief. They will be able to recover from the loss, and they will be happy again. They will continue to live happily ever after.

Where did the stages of grief come from?

The concept of grief comes from the Greek word "moeides," which means "suffering." In English, "grief" and "mourning" refer to two different feelings that arise in response to death. Grief is the emotional response to losing a loved one. Mourning is the process that involves the ritual of grieving. This ritual takes the form of rituals that the bereaved perform to honor the deceased or show respect for the deceased's life. So, how does this process come about?

When someone loses someone they love, they often experience a feeling of sadness. This is a natural reaction to their loss. It's an emotional response that all humans feel. Many people also feel anger, guilt, frustration, fear, loneliness, and despair. These feelings come from a person's loss of a loved one. But, some people also feel a sense of relief when their loved ones die. That is because they don't want to lose them. This feeling is called "grief." The feelings of grief are a natural response to the loss of someone you care about.

When we think of grief, we usually imagine it as a bad feeling that only people experience after losing someone they love. But, grief is more than that. Grief can be a positive feeling too. It's a normal feeling that we all feel sometimes. It comes from losing someone you care about. If you care for someone, it is normal to experience grief when they die. It can be a good feeling because you know that the person who has died is no longer suffering or feeling pain.

There are specific rules that you must follow when you are grieving. When you are suffering, you should avoid making unnecessary changes to your life. It's okay to change your diet, but it's not a good idea to cut back on sleep. It's also okay to stay with family members, but you shouldn't stay with them all day. You must find a time that works for you to spend alone. It's not good to stay home all day watching TV or reading. If you do that, you might get depressed.

You should be gentle with yourself. You don't have to do everything you want to do. You don't have to do anything you don't want to do. You should rest if you need to. It's also okay to take time off from work. Just don't do it too much. You don't want to burn out.

The feelings that you experience while grieving are normal. They will pass. As you continue to grieve, you'll eventually get over the feeling of grief. In the meantime, it's okay to be sad. You don't have to hide your sadness or pretend that you don't care. People can tell that you are sad, and they will understand.

As you're grieving, you shouldn't spend all of your time thinking about the person who died. It's also not a good idea to think about how terrible their death was. It's not necessary to worry about how the person who has died. It's good to remember the person who has died and the good times with them.

First, you must understand that mourning comes from a sense of loss. When you lose someone you care about, you feel sad, and you miss them. That is the first step in the process of mourning. Next, you begin thinking about the person who has died. You think about how they would react to certain situations in your life right now. When you are feeling sad, you should think about the deceased. This will make you feel better. You might think of happy memories that you have with the deceased.

You should think of the things that made you love them. Remember the things that you liked about them. Remember the things that they did for you. Thinking about the deceased will help you to feel better. This is the second step in the process of mourning. Finally, you have to remember the good times with the deceased. It would help if you thought about what you enjoyed doing together. Think about the moments when you were happy.

You can also think about the people who were close to the deceased. You can think about the time when the deceased was sick and the things that helped to make them feel better. This will help you to feel better as well. This is the third step in the process of mourning.

Does grief always follow the same order of stages?

As in art, we sometimes feel that things go out of order in life. In fact, there are specific times when this happens in grief. The order of grief, however, is not random. Grief has a natural order to its progression, and it follows a particular set of stages. Each person's grief will vary in length and intensity, but the progression of grief always follows the same order.

One thing that most of us can relate to is grieving over someone we loved. Many people feel that grief is not orderly. Some people think it should happen all at once, and it doesn't. However, that's not true. It really does follow a specific order.

When someone loses someone close to them, it usually takes time to accept the loss. Sometimes, we feel that it was too soon, too fast, or too sudden. This is normal. In fact, some people would want to rush into acceptance of this new reality, which can lead to depression. This doesn't mean that the feelings of grief aren't real, but it does mean that it's normal to take a little while to adjust to the loss. Once you do, you'll feel better. In fact, the people who think that they have to rush through the grief often end up feeling worse.

In life, we all experience grief at different times. Some things in life will bring us grief. For example, if a loved one dies, we might experience grief. The order in which we experience grief is the same for everyone. Grief has a mandate to it.

When we are going through grief, we follow a particular process.

Some people find that grieving is easier if they have someone to talk to, especially if they are close relatives or friends. The best time to deal with grief is right after the loss occurs. If you don't, you could feel guilty for not being able to cope with the loss. If you want to deal with your grief, remember not to dwell on it too long. Grieving is a natural process. Don't hold yourself back if you can't get over your loss in a week. Grieving is a process that takes time.

Grief is an inevitable part of life. When one dies, we feel a sense of loss. In order to deal with the loss, we need to deal with it by talking to our loved ones and friends. You might even find that it is good to get away from everything for a while to get some time to think about what has happened and how you are going to live your life from now on.

However, it would be best if you remembered that grieving is different for everybody. One day you may feel better than another. Sometimes it helps to share your feelings with others. It could even help to visit a counselor if you have trouble dealing with your grief. A counselor could offer you valuable advice that could help you overcome your grief.

Going through the 5 stages of grief: How does it feel?

You might think this is a silly question, but it's essential to understand what is meant by the term "grief." Grief is basically the process of moving from happiness or joy to sadness or pain. You go through these five stages of grief when you face a loss or a loss-like situation. This is a part of life where you learn about how people react to loss and how you can adapt to them.

You've probably heard about the five stages of grief, but what does it really mean? Well, it's a way of understanding why people react the way they do when faced with specific traumatic events. The theory is based on the idea that humans naturally react to grief and loss in one of five distinct phases, each of which has its own set of emotions and responses.

There are five stages of grief, and they are natural responses to loss. Going through the five stages of grief is a normal and natural part of any human life. Whether you are dealing with a friend or family member that has passed away, the loss of a loved one, or the loss of a close friend. When going through any loss, there is usually a period where the feelings and emotions of the person are not felt or understood. This is when the person is going through the five stages of grief.

When we are faced with loss, we feel confused and sad. We also feel angry, and we may blame ourselves for the loss. We may even think we are the reason the loss happened. We may try to find reasons to justify why the person died. We are also more vulnerable to other people's negative comments. We tend to avoid people we know caused the loss.

We might become isolated as we try to figure out what to do. We don't want to face our loss, we don't want to talk about it, we don't want to think about it, and we don't want to feel anything. We don't want to feel anything because we believe that feeling nothing is better than feeling our feelings. It's also hard to think about how to handle the loss.

When we are in this stage, we may become depressed and isolate ourselves. We may feel helpless and hopeless. We might think that the only way to deal with the loss is to forget it. We may also start thinking about revenge. We may become preoccupied with the guilt of what we did to cause the loss. We may become obsessed with how we could have done something to prevent the loss.

Each stage has its own emotions and responses. For instance, when a person loses a loved one, they are likely to feel anger towards the dead person for a while after the death. However, this stage usually ends after a few days, and the person is left feeling numb or empty. After this point, there will be a phase where the person experiences guilt and remorse. They will also experience sadness and loneliness, and eventually, they will come to terms with the death.

If you are going through any loss and it has caused you to feel sad, it is important to try and work through the different stages of grief. Once you have come to the end of the cycle of the five stages, you will feel better.

Grief is a normal response to the death of a loved one. It is the process of moving from happiness or elation to sadness or pain. You go through these five stages of grief when you face a loss or a loss-like situation. You can use this as a guideline to help you understand why people react the way they do when faced with certain traumatic events. It's a part of life where you learn about how people respond to loss and how you can adapt to them.

The Five Stages Of Grief

Grief is a natural process that we go through after losing someone we love. There are five stages that most people go through during their grief journey: denial, anger, bargaining, depression, and acceptance. Each stage can last for a different amount of time. Still, eventually, the person will reach acceptance and be able to move on.

You can expect that people will experience these emotions for a while after they have lost someone close to them. You can expect that people will experience these emotions for a certain length of time. After this period has ended, people should be able to move on and feel better.

It is essential to realize that grief is not a sign of weakness. On the contrary, it is actually a very human emotion. We are all capable of having feelings and expressing them. Grief is an essential and normal emotion that we can feel at any time in our lives. It is a part of being human, and it can help us cope with our losses.

It's important to understand that grief is a normal part of being human. It's a part of life, and it's something we all go through at some point. When we lose someone close to us, we will probably have to deal with this feeling. People go through five stages of grief. The five stages are denial, anger, bargaining, depression, and acceptance. Some people experience all five stages, while others only go through the first three.

Denial is the first stage, where people deny experiencing any problems. Anger is the second stage, where people become outraged. Bargaining is the third stage, where people develop a plan to try to solve the problem. Depression is the fourth stage, where people feel sad and depressed. Acceptance is the final stage, where people realize that the loss is inevitable and will have to deal with it.

Stage One: Denial

The denial stage of grief is the hardest to deal with. It's when you first realize that your loved one is gone, but you can't accept it. You may try to pretend that they are still alive or that everything will be okay. Denial is a natural reaction to the tragedy, and it's important to remember that it doesn't mean you're wrong about what happened. It's just a way of coping with the pain until you can accept the reality of your loss.

Denial is the act of refusing to acknowledge or accept a truth or reality. It can be an effective coping mechanism for dealing with difficult emotions. People use denial to avoid pain and uncomfortable truths. Denial can be helpful when faced with overwhelming evidence that disproves a person's beliefs. Some people use denial to avoid facing their vulnerabilities.

The denial stage of grief is when a person denies that they are grieving. They may act like everything is normal or like they are in control. They may not want to talk about their feelings or go to therapy. They may have a hard time going to the funeral home. They may not cry. They may be angry and bitter. People who are in denial usually don't want to deal with their grief, so they try to ignore it.

Denial is a typical response to a traumatic event. It's the stage of grief where people try to push the unpleasant memories away and think more positively. But how long does denial last? And is it healthy to stay in denial? Experts say that denial can be helpful at first, but it can cause problems over time.

In general, experts recommend that people go through the stages of grief healthily and finally accept their loss. For example, it can keep people from seeking help or facing their emotions head-on. And if someone doesn't deal with their denial eventually, it can lead to depression or other mental health issues.

Denial is a typical stage of grief. It's characterized by a refusal to accept the loss, despite clear evidence to the contrary. Denial can manifest itself in a wide range of ways. Still, some common symptoms include: feeling out of control, refusing to talk about the death, being emotionally numb, and not being able to think or focus on anything else. It's important to remember that denial isn't an indicator of strength—it's just a way of coping with pain in an unhealthy way.

Many people experience grief in different ways and at other times. But there are some general signs that you or someone you know may be in the denial stage of grief. Denial usually starts with disbelief, anger, bargaining, and acceptance. In the denial stage, a person may not want to face facts about their loss or may push away anyone who tries to help them. They may also avoid thinking about the deceased or feeling emotional about them. Denial usually has a negative effect on your life. It may make you feel angry, sad, depressed, hopeless, or guilty.

Denial is a common response to grief. It can be helpful in the early stages of grieving when the emotions are intense, and there is little room for anything else. But denial can eventually become a barrier to recovery. Denial can keep you from accepting that your loved one is gone, preventing you from moving on. It can also lead to problems with intimacy and other relationships. If you're in the denial stage of grief, it's essential to talk about it with someone who understands how you're feeling.

Denial is a common reaction to grief. It's the stage of grief where the person doesn't believe that their loved one is gone or that their loved one's death was real. Denial can prevent people from dealing with the pain of loss. There are ways to deal with denial, though. One way is to talk about your feelings with someone else. Another way is to write about your feelings. Finally, try to take some time for yourself and do things that make you happy.

Grief is an emotion that is felt after a loss. The denial stage of grief is when the person does not want to believe that their loved one is gone. This stage can last for weeks or months. During the denial stage, the person may not want to see or talk to anyone about their loss. They may also be angry and refuse to get help. Eventually, the person will reach the acceptance stage of grief. At this point, they will start to deal with their feelings and begin to heal.

Stage Two: Anger

It can be challenging to distinguish between anger and grief at first, but there are some key distinctions to keep in mind. Anger is a natural and normal feeling when we experience pain or trauma. Anger typically lasts for a relatively short period and is fueled by our need to lash out at those who have hurt us in the past. Grief is an intense, prolonged, and sometimes uncontrollable emotion that follows the death of a loved one.

Anger is a common emotion people experience during the grief stage. It can help deal with negative emotions, such as sadness and regret. Some people use anger as a way to cope with their grief. Anger allows people to feel stronger and more in control. It also helps them focus on what they want and need instead of dwelling on their losses. Anger is a common emotion during the grieving process.

It is natural to feel anger when you lose someone you love. Grieving doesn't always go smoothly, and people often experience difficult emotions, such as anger, in different stages. The anger stage of grief is a normal part of the process and shouldn't be ignored or suppressed. Expressing your anger constructively can help you deal with your feelings and move on from your loss.

The anger stage of grief is the feeling that comes after a loss. It can be a confusing and frustrating time for those going through it. This stage can last for months or even years and involve many different emotions. People in the anger stage may feel angry, frustrated, bitter, and resentful. They may also feel like they're constantly on guard and never able to relax.

Anger is a common emotion during the grieving process. However, it usually lasts for only a few weeks. After that, people start to feel sadness and depression again. The anger stage of grief is sometimes referred to as the "hurt" stage. It's not uncommon for people to feel angry and upset after a loss. Most people feel angry at first, but they don't stay in this stage very long. They may even feel guilty that they're angry.

Why do people get angry during the grieving process? People can feel angry at someone they love, even if they aren't around to hurt them anymore. Some people may feel angry because they're afraid their loved ones will come back from the grave to haunt or harm them.

People may become irritable, hostile, and argumentative. They may lash out at family and friends or become withdrawn and isolate themselves. They may also have trouble sleeping or concentrating. They may feel nervous and tense, have headaches or stomach problems, or have a pounding heart. They may also experience chest pains, high blood pressure, or anxiety attacks.

How is the anger stage of grief different from the sadness and guilt stages? The anger stage usually comes after the sadness and guilt. However, some people may experience it simultaneously as in other stages. The anger stage is not as severe as the depression. It's also not as long-lasting. People with the anger stage of grief can usually get through their grief more quickly than people with depression.

Some telltale signs that a person may be in the anger stage of grief include feeling overwhelmed and frequently lashing out at those around them. Individuals in this phase often feel an intense sense of betrayal and anger towards the deceased, making it difficult for them to cope. If you or someone you know seems to be experiencing these symptoms, it may be good to seek out professional help.

Anger is often destructive and leads to poor decision-making. It is essential for those going through grief to be aware of the risks to make informed decisions about how best to cope. Anger can be a symptom of depression, which is an illness that is best treated by a medical professional. Anger can also lead to substance abuse and poor decision-making.

Anger is a natural response to grief, but it shouldn't be tolerated or acted on. Here are some tips for dealing with anger during the anger stage:

- Recognize that anger is part of the grieving process and isn't something to be ashamed of. It's normal to feel angry and frustrated, and there's nothing wrong with healthily expressing that anger.
- Talk about your feelings with someone you trust. Talking about how you're feeling can help alleviate some of the pain and frustration you may be feeling.
- Be patient with yourself. Don't expect to get over your grief overnight or without putting in some effort. Take things slow and don't rush through challenging moments in order to move on quickly.
- Remember that grieving doesn't have to be a lonely experience.

Anger is a natural reaction to grief. It's a way of expressing our frustration and anger, and it can help us cope with the pain of losing someone. But eventually, we have to let go of that anger. We have to learn to forgive ourselves and those who hurt us. And we have to find hope again. The majority of those who experience the death of a loved one will eventually move through all of these stages. It may take some time, but they will get there.

Stage Three: Bargaining

Grieving is a process that will vary from person to person. People who are experiencing the grieving process may try to get their loved ones back by doing anything possible. This can include begging, pleading, and even blackmail. In the bargaining stage of grief, people may try to get their loved ones back by doing anything possible. Sometimes, people may feel like they need their loved ones to come back in order to feel complete again. While this may be true for some people, it is not always the case.

The bargaining stage is when people start to bargain with God for their loved one's return. They may ask for their loved ones to come back or ask for forgiveness. People use the bargaining stage to try and make sense of what has happened and find a way to move on. Bargaining with God is common for people who hope their loved ones will come back. They may start by praying, asking for forgiveness, and offering sacrifices.

The bargaining stage of grief is when people start to look for ways to get back to their previous life. This can be when people make decisions that may not be in their best interest, such as staying in an abusive relationship or drinking excessively. It's important to remember that bargaining isn't always imperfect; sometimes, it's a sign that someone is trying to cope healthily. It's also important to remember that the bargaining stage doesn't last forever.

The bargaining stage of grief varies people from the person. The person is trying to find a way to work through the pain and start moving on with their life. They may try to bargain with God, themselves, or others about how long they have to grieve. They may also bargain with time, trying to speed up the process so they can move on. They may also feel that they need to bargain with God about the future. They may wish to stop grieving as soon as possible, or they may want to endure the process of mourning.

The bargaining stage of grief is a common experience after a loss. It is characterized by irritability, anger, and a need for control. People in the bargaining stage may be pressured to hurry the grieving process or find a "fix" for their pain. They may also feel resentful or angry towards those around them. The bargaining stage of grief is often accompanied by severe depression.

People in the bargaining stage of grief may complain that they feel "down" or have lost their energy. They may be preoccupied with the loss or re-live the experience repeatedly. They may also feel guilty about their feelings and make promises to themselves not to feel this way again. The bargaining stage of grief is typically short-lived. Depression is a common symptom of the bargaining stage of grief. In fact, up to 25% of people in this stage may suffer from depression. This can be a challenging time for children grieving the loss of a parent or other loved one.

A person in the bargaining stage of grief may:

- Be preoccupied with details of the lost loved ones, such as where they were when they died, what they were wearing, or their possessions.
- Display a solid need to understand and resolve the death somehow.
- Argumentative and non-compliant behavior with friends and family members.
- Experiencing mood swings, such as being overly happy or sad for no apparent reason.
- Pushing away loved ones who try to comfort them.
- Seeking out others who have lost a loved one and sharing their loss with them.

- Having difficulty concentrating or sleeping, or being unusually irritable.

The bargaining stage of grief is a natural and expected process that helps people adjust to a loss. However, bargaining risks are associated, which can hinder the healing process. People who bargain may feel like they're not given enough time or attention to their feelings and maybe pushed to move on from their loss quickly.

This can cause them to feel resentful or angry, further impeding the grieving process. It's crucial for those going through the bargaining stage of grief to be aware of these risks and make sure loved ones and professionals support them.

First, it's essential to understand that bargaining is a natural process that occurs during the grieving process. Bargaining reflects our need to maintain control and make decisions under challenging circumstances. However, bargaining can also be destructive and can lead to feelings of anger and frustration. It is important to remember that bargaining does not mean getting what you want at all costs; it means finding a mutually acceptable solution.

Here are some tips for managing the bargaining stage of grief:

- Recognize that bargaining is a natural process and allow yourself to engage in it. Try not to get too wrapped up in trying to win or lose the negotiation. Instead, focus on finding an agreement that you can live with.
- Keep communication open throughout the negotiation process. Talking about your thoughts and feelings will help reduce tension and build trust.
- Remember that bargaining is a time for you to resolve your feelings about the situation. Many people find it

helpful to write down their thoughts and feelings and wish to work through them. It can be especially helpful if a friend or relative encourages you to write down your wishes.

After the bargaining stage of grief, many people feel a sense of relief. They have moved on from the intense pain and sadness that led them to seek professional help in the first place. However, there is still work to be done. People must remember to forgive themselves and others for their role in causing the death of a loved one. Finding closure is vital in order to move on with life.

Stage Four: Depression

There are many different stages of grief. The "depression stage" is a very common one that often lasts for several months or even years. During this stage, you may feel very sad and down all the time. You may have trouble sleeping or concentrating, and you may have a lot of thoughts about suicide. It's important to remember that you're not alone in your feelings during this stage, and help is available.

There is no definitive answer when it comes to what the depression stage of grief is, and as such, it can vary from person to person. However, some general themes tend to be common among those who experience this stage. These include feeling overwhelmed by the death, experiencing a loss of appetite and/or sleep, feeling like nothing will ever feel good again, and feeling like a constant voice in the back of their head telling them that they are responsible for their loved ones one's death.

It can be challenging to navigate through this stage, but it is essential to remember that everyone experiences grief in their own unique way. Many people also experience depression during the grieving process. Those who have experienced this stage of grief often feel like they are a different person than they were before the death of their loved ones. They may experience many negative emotions, including anger, irritability, sadness, and shame.

Coping with depression in the grief stage of recovery is similar to how you would cope with it during any other period of life. In the depression stage, you may feel overwhelmed by sadness and loneliness and experience difficulty concentrating or sleeping. It's important not to ignore or push away these feelings because they only show that your grief is recycled correctly. You can learn to recognize when you are depressed and take care of yourself by seeking professional help if necessary.

When someone dies, the process of grieving can last anywhere from a few days to several months or even years. The length of time it takes to go through the stages of grief is individualized and can vary depending on the person's history, personality, and relationship with the deceased. However, there are some general guidelines that most people follow during the grieving process.

The depression stage of grief typically lasts approximately 6-8 months. It is characterized by various symptoms such as feeling numb, loss of interest in previously enjoyable activities, and feelings of hopelessness and despair. The stages of grief also include the routine physical, emotional, and cognitive stages.

The physical stage of grief is characterized by increased appetite, weight gain or loss, and sleeping problems.

The emotional stage of grief includes a variety of symptoms, including general irritability and anger, but also sadness, depression, and guilt.

The cognitive stage of grief is characterized by memory problems, intrusive thoughts, newfound interest in the deceased, and feelings of helplessness.

Depression is a common symptom of the grief stage. It can be a sign that you are feeling overwhelmed and sad. Other symptoms of depression may include: feeling empty or numb, having trouble concentrating, sleeping too much or not enough, losing interest in activities you used to enjoy, feeling irritable or angry, and having thoughts about suicide. If you are experiencing any of these symptoms, it is important to talk to your doctor or therapist about them.

If you or someone you know is in the depression stage of grief, there are some key signs to look for. One significant indicator is that the individual is drastically changing their behavior. They may stop eating or sleeping, become withdrawn and isolate themselves from friends and family, and have trouble concentrating or making decisions.

In some cases, these changes can be dramatic and lead to feelings of extreme sadness, guilt, and anger. If you notice any of these symptoms in a loved one after a loss, it's important to reach out for help. There are support groups available that can provide guidance through this difficult time.

Depression is a common complication following bereavement. It is estimated that up to 25% of bereaved people experience at least one bout of major depression. The risk of developing depression increases with the duration and severity of the bereavement experience and with age, gender, and marital status. Women are more likely than men to experience major depression after bereavement. However, the reasons for this disparity are unknown.

A number of risk factors have been identified for the development of depression in general, including a history of mental illness or suicide attempts, a lack of social support, and exposure to traumatic events. Depression may also be associated with poorer physical health outcomes, such as an increased risk for cardiovascular disease and mortality.

Other social and environmental factors that may contribute to the development of depression in bereaved spouses include a lack of support from friends and family, inadequate financial resources, and the presence of chronic illness. Despite the extensive research on risk factors, no definitive causal link has been established.

Depression is a very common side effect of grief. Sometimes people feel sad and hopeless for months or even years after a death. It's important to know that there are things you can do to help deal with depression. Many self-help books and websites are available that can provide helpful advice. Talk to your doctor or mental health professional about what you need, and don't hesitate to ask for help.

Eventually, most people move on from the depression stage and begin to rebuild their lives. Here are some tips for getting through the depression stage:

- Talk about your feelings with others. It can be helpful to share your experiences and feelings with a trusted friend or family member.
- Get plenty of rest. Sleep is essential for restoration and healing, so make sure to get enough restorative sleep.
- Exercise regularly. Exercise can boost moods and help clear out negative thoughts and emotions.

- Keep a journal. Writing helps you make sense of your feelings and can help you cope with the grief experience.
- Attend support groups. Support groups provide a safe place to talk about your experiences and get helpful advice from others who have been there before.

Stage Five: Acceptance

Grief is a natural, healthy process that leads to healing. During the acceptance stage, survivors are able to come to terms with their loss and begin the process of rebuilding their lives. It is essential for them to remember that they are not alone in this journey and that there is hope. It is also important to remember that often, the ways in which a person grieves will vary.

Acceptance can be an extremely challenging period for many people. This is a common reaction to grief. Many survivors try to avoid the feelings of grief, focusing instead on moving forward and not dwelling on the past. In addition, survivors often try to change how they feel about their losses by finding new hobbies and interests. Some survivors may use alcohol or drugs to cope with grief.

The acceptance stage is the last step of grief, and it's when people start to accept that their loved one is gone. They may feel sadness, emptiness, and guilt, but they're also starting to move on. Acceptance is necessary because it allows people to begin rebuilding their lives. Once they accept their losses, they can begin the process of grieving healthily.

The acceptance stage of grief is the process that individuals go through after losing a loved one. It can look different for everyone, but it usually includes coming to terms with the loss and feeling some level of closure. Some people may feel numb or empty at this stage, while others may experience heightened emotions. The acceptance stage can take weeks, months, or even years, but eventually, everyone reaches a point where they move on from the death of their loved one.

The acceptance stage of grief typically lasts between 6 and 12 months. This is the time when you start to accept that the person who died is gone and that life will never be the same again. You may feel numb at first, but gradually you will start to feel a range of emotions, including sadness, loneliness, and anger. It can be challenging to cope with these feelings, but you will eventually reach a point where you can move on by working through them.

When you are in the acceptance stage of grief, there are some things you need to remember. Your grief is different from others. It will be a mixture of your feelings and memories. You will experience sadness, anger, and loneliness. These feelings may seem overwhelming at first, but they will eventually pass. You may feel numb, but this will give as well. You will want to speak to other people who are experiencing grief, but you need to be careful that you don't blame or criticize them. This is not the time for blaming others or feeling angry with them.

The acceptance stage of grief is when a person begins to accept that their loved one has died and that they will never see them again. This can be a complex process, as many people don't want to believe that their loved one is gone. Some common symptoms of the acceptance stage of grief are feeling numb, being detached from others, and having difficulty concentrating. It is important to remember that this is a natural process and not to rush through it.

When these symptoms start to pass, you will be able to feel much better. You will begin to care about others again and feel like you are a part of the world again. Eventually, you may even be able to get back to everyday life.

The acceptance stage of grief is when the person who is grieving has accepted that their loved one is gone and they are moving on. They may feel sadness and emptiness, but they have also acknowledged that the loved one is gone and there is nothing they can do to bring them back. Some common symptoms of being in the acceptance stage of grief include feeling better overall after a period of intense sadness, finding new ways to spend time alone, adjusting quickly to changes in routine, and feeling emotionally stable.

It can take months or years for someone to go through all of the stages of grief, but once they reach the acceptance stage, they are more likely to live a whole life without their loved one. The death of a loved one can be upsetting and unpredictable, and it can take time for the survivor to get used to their new situation.

The acceptance stage of grief is a time of change and adjustment for those who are grieving. It can be difficult because it is unfamiliar territory, and there are many risks associated with it. The risk of being alone during this period is greater than the risk of not having support. The most important thing to remember during this stage is that you are not alone, and help is available.

If you feel lost and confused, you can get help to guide you through the acceptance stage. You can find a grief counselor at the National Grief Center. If you feel lost and confused, ask your friends or family for help to guide you through the acceptance stage of grief. They will be happy to assist you.

Grieving isn't a process that ends when the person who has died is buried. Grieving can continue long after the funeral or cremation, and it can be a difficult and challenging journey. Here are some tips to help you through the acceptance stage of grief:

- Acknowledge that grief is normal and natural. Everyone experiences loss in their own way, so don't compare your experience to anyone else's.
- Talk about your feelings with someone you trust. Talking about your thoughts and feelings will help ease the burden and make you feel better understood.
- Try to take some time for yourself each day to do something that brings you joy, even if it's just for a few minutes. This will help you center yourself and stay on track during this difficult time.
- Don't beat yourself up for feeling sad or angry. It's perfectly normal to feel these emotions, but you mustn't let them control you.
- Look forward to being able to share your life with your loved one again.

Many questions remain after someone has gone through the acceptance stage of grief. Some people feel like they need to do something to move on, while others find that they just need time to process everything. Here are some of the most common questions:

- When is the best time to start rebuilding relationships?
- Should you keep all of your possessions from before death?
- How can you tell if you're still in the acceptance stage?
- What should you do if a loved one won't let go?

You don't need to answer all these questions right away. If you've just experienced the death of a loved one, you may feel like you need to take action right away. However, this isn't always the case. The acceptance stage is continuous progress. It's normal to feel upset, angry, or despairing at first. But in reality, there's no perfect time to say goodbye. You might want to move on sooner if your loved one's death was sudden and unexpected.

Other Possible Stages of Grief:

Different people go through various stages of grief in the aftermath of a loved one's death. Some may only experience one stage, while others may go through several. Regardless of the order in which they occur, these are the five stages: denial, anger, bargaining, depression, and finally, acceptance.

In some cases, it is believed that healing is also a stage of grief. The grieving process never ends and can be a long and arduous journey for many people. It is important to remember that there is no one right way to go through this experience and that everyone experiences the grieving process differently.

There are many ways to cope with grief, including talking about your feelings with friends and family, seeking professional help, practicing yoga or meditation, writing in your journal, or using art as a form of expression. Although it may feel challenging at times, enduring the grieving process is ultimately beneficial for you and those around you.

There are many possible stages of grief, and not all people experience the same five. Some people may only experience one or two stages, while others may go through multiple stages over time. Whatever the case may be, it's important to understand that not everyone goes through the same process when grieving. In fact, there are other possible stages of grief that are often overlooked.

When you're grieving, it's essential to be aware of the different stages of grief and understand how each one affects you. Each stage is unique in its own way, but they all share certain commonalities that make them similar. So while it's important to be aware of the stages of grief, it's also important to be aware of all stages.

Common misconceptions about grieving

Grieving is a process that can take many different forms. It is not always easy to understand what goes on during the grieving process, especially if you don't have experience with it. There are some common misconceptions about grieving that people often hold onto, even when they may not be accurate. Here are five of the most common ones:

I am doing it wrong.

There are many misconceptions about grieving. People think they should be doing something specific when they're grieving or that there is a fixed timeline for how long it will take them to heal. In reality, healing from grief takes time and varies from person to person. Additionally, people often believe that if they don't show their sadness or anger, then they're not actually grieving.

However, expressing emotions is an essential part of the healing process. When people suppress their feelings and bury them, they may feel even worse at a later date. The first step to moving forward from a loss is to talk about it with someone and let it go.

I should be feeling...

There's a misconception that one should feel happy and joyous during the grieving process. However, this is not always the case for those who have lost a loved one.

Grieving can be very painful and challenging, and it can take a long time to heal. Some people may feel sad, depressed, or angry during the process. It is important to remember that everyone grieves differently, and there is no right or wrong way to feel.

You shouldn't be ashamed of any of your feelings through the grieving process. It is normal to feel sad, angry, or frustrated. You should not be afraid to talk with others and ask them how they are feeling. This can be an excellent way to figure out what you're experiencing and how to cope with it.

This goes first

If you are grieving the loss of a loved one, it is essential to follow these guidelines during the first six months after their death: eat well, exercise, get plenty of sleep, avoid drugs and alcohol, and spend time with friends and family.

It's important to remember that grief doesn't come first. The healing process comes first. Grieving is a natural process that allows you to release the pain and sadness you feel after a loss. It can take time to get through the grieving process, but it is important to remember that it will eventually end. There are many ways to help support yourself during this time, including talking to someone about what you're going through, spending time with loved ones who care for you, and engaging in activities that make you happy.

My grief is taking too long.

There seems to be a misconception that grief is a finite and manageable emotion. In reality, grief can take many different forms and often lasts an indefinite amount of time. There are no right or wrong periods to deal with grief, as each experiences it in their own way.

There is no right amount of time to grieve a loss. Everyone has different coping skills, so that grieving can take different lengths of time for each person. It is important to remember that you're doing the best you can, even if it feels like it's taking forever. Grieving should be a personal process that allows you to explore your feelings and process what has happened. You shouldn't feel obligated to get through it all in a certain amount of time; instead, allow yourself the space and time you need to heal.

I'm depressed

The misconception that depression is simply a result of grieving is rampant in our society. While it's true that depression can be a side effect of grief, there is more to the story. Depression is a severe mental illness that can be caused by any number of factors, including genetics and environment. Left untreated, it can lead to suicide or other tragic consequences. So if you're feeling down, don't confuse your depressive symptoms with mourning; get help from a professional.

It can be caused by things like grief, stress, or trauma, but it's not always easy to know what's responsible for your feelings of sadness and despair. If you're depressed because of the grief you're experiencing, don't blame yourself. It's possible to develop depression even if you're not alone in your pain.

There are plenty of resources available to help you get through this difficult time.

When to reach out for help

If someone experiences a loss, they may go through different stages of grief. The first stage is denial. In this stage, the person may not believe that the loss has happened and may try to avoid thinking about it. The second stage is anger. This is when the person may feel resentment and anger towards the person or thing that caused the loss. The third stage is bargaining. In this stage, the person may try to find a way to get back what was lost or to get something else in return for it. The fourth stage is depression. This is when the person may feel sadness and hopelessness over the loss. The fifth stage is acceptance. In this stage, the person may finally accept that the loss has happened and move on with their life.

Grief is a natural response to loss. It is a combination of sadness, loneliness, and concern for the deceased. The grieving process can be different for every person, but it usually lasts about six months. During this time, people may feel intense sorrow, emptiness, and guilt. They may also have thoughts about the deceased that they cannot shake. Grieving is not always easy, but it is essential to remember that it is normal to feel these feelings after a loss.

When someone dies, the first and most important thing is to grieve. Grief is a natural process that helps us come to terms with the loss of a loved one. There is no right or wrong way to grieve; each person experiences grief in their own way. However, some common signs suggest it may be time to seek professional help.
These include: feeling isolated from others, experiencing intense mood swings, feeling overwhelmed by sadness, finding it difficult to concentrate on anything else, having

thoughts of suicide, and becoming preoccupied with the person's death. If you notice any of these signs affecting your quality of life or your ability to function normally, please reach out for help.

Grief is a natural and normal response to the death of a loved one. However, not everyone experiences grief in the same way. Some people may feel numb or isolated, while others may experience overwhelming sadness and sorrow. There are many ways to cope with grief, and seeking professional help is sometimes helpful. There are many resources available, including support groups and counselling services. It's important to find what works best for you and talk about your feelings with someone who can understand them.

Seek Help From Friends and Family

If you are experiencing personal difficulties, it may be helpful to talk to friends and family about what is going on. They can provide a listening ear and support system, making all the difference when struggling with complex issues. Consider reaching out for help in the following ways:

- Talking to someone you trust about what's been going on can be incredibly helpful in terms of relieving some of the stress that comes with difficult experiences.
- Confiding in a loved one can also lead to feelings of empowerment and healing.
- Consider seeking professional help from a therapist, counselor, or psychiatrist if things seem to be getting out of hand or if there are persistent issues that prevent you from functioning at your best.

- Speaking with a support group can offer valuable insight and support as you navigate these challenging times.

Seek Help From Support Groups

If you're feeling lost in the aftermath of a loved one's death, support groups are available to help. Grieving can be a lonely experience, but groups offer an opportunity to share your experiences and receive support from others who are going through what you are. Support groups can also provide resources and ideas for coping with grief. You might also find that a support group can offer comfort and insight without making you feel judged or inadequate.

Seek Help From Mental Health Professionals

Some people find it difficult to cope with their grief. If you are struggling with your grief, you may want to consider seeking help from a therapist or counselor. A therapist can offer you advice on dealing with your feelings and can provide support during this difficult time. A therapist can also help you learn how to cope with grief in the long term, helping you to look forward and move on.

In conclusion, grief can be complicated to cope with on your own. If you are experiencing grief, it is essential to seek help from a professional.
In conclusion, grief can be very difficult to cope with on your own. Grieving involves a process of sorting through emotions and adjusting to new life circumstances. It can be helpful to talk about your feelings with someone who

understands what you're going through. Many resources are available to help people cope with grief, including support groups, counseling, and books. If you're feeling overwhelmed, emergency services can also assist.

How to help someone who is grieving?

Grief is a natural response to loss. We feel an emotion when something important to us has been taken away or when we have experienced a loss. Grief can be difficult to deal with, but it is a necessary process that helps us heal. Grief has been called many things. To some people, grief is simply the way they feel when losing someone they love. To others, grief is a term used to describe the pain that comes with loss.

Many people believe that there are right and wrong ways to grieve. However, this is not the case. Grieving is a personal process that should be tailored to the individual. There is no one right way to grieve, but there are many commonalities among different grieving styles. Some people may prefer to keep their mourning private, while others may want to share their experiences with the world. Ultimately, what matters most is how each person processes their grief.

There are many things people can do to help someone who is grieving. Some people may want to offer their support through words, while others may want to provide tangible help such as cooking meals or cleaning up. Everyone needs to remember that grieving is an individual process and what works for one person may not work for another. However, some general tips can help support someone through their grief.

When someone loses a loved one, they may feel bewildered and lost. In addition to grieving the loss of the person themselves, family and friends often need to provide support during this time. Here are some tips you can help someone who is grieving:

- Listen without judgment. It can be hard to open up about our feelings, but hearing someone else's story helps us understand what they're going through.
- Offer support during the earliest stages of grief. This might mean providing emotional support, listening attentively, or simply being there for a hug when needed.
- Avoid making assumptions about how long it will take to grieve. Everyone experiences grief differently, and there is no one right way to go through the process.
- Respect the privacy of the grieving person. It can be hard to understand why someone would want to hide their pain or avoid being seen, but it's important to respect the grieving person's privacy.
- Don't try to "fix" someone's grief. The grieving process is personal, and upsetting or aggravating the person won't help them heal.

Grief is a complex process, but there are ways to help make it a little bit easier. Many people find comfort in talking about their feelings, and there are many support groups available to help those who are grieving. It is important to remember that grief is an individual experience, and what works for one person may not work for another. People may have strong reactions to death and be upset for a long time. The most important thing is to remember that these feelings are normal and that everyone experiences grief in their own way.

How Long Is Too Long to Mourn?

Mourning is a natural process that helps us cope with the death of a loved one. But how long should we mourn? Some people believe that mourning should last for a period of 6 months, while others say it can last for up to two years. Ultimately, it is up to the individual to decide how long they need to grieve. We need to look at the natural process of mourning as a way to cope with the death of a loved one.

If you're struggling to mourn the death of a loved one, there are a few things you can do to help. First, it's important to remember that no one is immune from grief. Everyone goes through different stages of mourning, and everyone deals with death in their own way.

If you feel like you're stuck in a particular stage or that your mourning isn't going as well as you'd like, talk to someone about what you're experiencing. It can be helpful to have another perspective or someone who can offer encouragement and support. Additionally, try writing about your thoughts and feelings on grief in a journal or other private space. This can allow you to process your grief individually and share your thoughts with others who might be interested in hearing them.

Mourning is a natural process that helps us deal with the death of someone we love. It can take different forms, depending on how closely we were connected to the person who died. If you're not sure when you're ready to move on from mourning, here are six signs that you may be ready:

- You've accepted that your loved one is gone and moved on with your life.

- You have stopped dwelling on the past and are focusing on the present and future.
- You had stopped comparing yourself to how you were before they died and have started living in the present moment.
- You no longer feel guilty or ashamed about your feelings or actions related to mourning.
- You've decided that it's time to start dating again and enjoy life again.
- You have accepted that you can't change the past, and you are no longer replaying it in your mind.

Moving on from a loss can be a complicated process, but there are some simple steps you can take to speed up the process. Here are some tips to help you get started:

- Be patient. Grieving takes time, and it may not happen overnight. Give yourself time to adjust and process what has happened. Cry when you need to cry, but don't push yourself to snap out of the mourning phase too quickly.
- Talk about your loss with loved ones. Discussing your feelings openly will help relieve some of the pain and allow you to start moving on. Hearing other people's perspectives can also help build understanding and support for your journey through grief.
- Create a support system. Finding friends or family members who will listen without judging is crucial during this time. You can only take so much for yourself before you need to share your pain with others. If you feel like you need an emotional outlet, reach out to a close friend or family member who can help you release the tension from your day-to-day life.

- Remember that you are not alone. You have an entire community behind you, which can help strengthen you and give you the strength to manage your grief healthily. The more support you can receive from family, friends, and loved ones, the easier it will be to heal.
- Remember that you are human, and we all make mistakes. You are not alone in this life, no matter what circumstances you may be going through at this time. We all have a story, and we all have our fair share of ups and downs.

In conclusion, mourning is a personal process that can take on many different forms, and there is no set time limit for how long it should last. Some people may feel the need to grieve for a period of months or even years, while others may only need a few weeks or months. Ultimately, it is up to the individual how long they want to spend mourning their loss.

Living With Grief

Grief is something that everyone will experience at some point in their life. It can come as a reaction to a loss, such as the death of a loved one, or it may be a gradual process that develops over time. Regardless of when it strikes, grief is an unavoidable part of life. Below are tips that can help you for living with grief:

- Allow yourself to grieve in your own way. There is no one right way to deal with grief, and what works for one person may not work for another. What matters most is that you allow yourself to feel the emotions that come with it.

- Don't bottle up your feelings. Grief can be emotional and overwhelming, leading to feelings of guilt or shame if they're not appropriately expressed. It's important to talk about your feelings with someone who will understand and support you.

- Don't avoid the subject of death. Death is a reality, and it can be challenging to talk about. It's essential to be able to get your feelings out and share them with others so that you feel supported in dealing with them.

- Don't overdo it. It's important to be able to let go of things, but it's equally important not to lose yourself in your grief. Remember that grief is a process and that you need time to heal.

- Don't expect too much from others. Grief is a very personal process, and no one else can really understand what you're going through. It's not reasonable to expect people to change their behavior and be more understanding.

- Don't feel guilty about grieving. Grief is a normal part of life. It's okay to feel sad or angry about losing a loved one.

There is no right or wrong way to go through the five stages of grief, but there are some general guidelines that can help you move through them more effectively. The five stages are denial, anger, bargaining, depression, and acceptance. It's vital to get you through them to move on. Acceptance is the final stage of grief, and it can be the hardest. It takes time to accept a loss fully, but you must move through the stages to reach this point.

People experience grief in different ways and at different times. Some people may feel intense sadness and loneliness, while others may find relief from the pain. Whatever the case may be, it is essential to find what works best for you. There are some things you can try to help cope with grief.

Get support from family and friends. Talk about your feelings and let them know how they can help. They may also be able to provide advice on dealing with the grieving process. Participate in activities that make you happy or remind you of the person who died. It can be helpful to do something each day that pleases you, whether it's reading a book, going for a walk, or spending time with loved ones. Avoid worrying about the future or dwelling on the past too much.

There are many ways to remember a loved one who has passed away. Some people choose to have a memorial service or burial, while others may choose to keep the person's ashes or personal belongings as a reminder of their life. Whatever choice someone makes, it is important to remember the loved one in their own way, which means being comfortable with what feels right for them.

When a loved one dies, it can be incredibly difficult to cope. Friends and family members often feel helpless and alone in their grief. There is not always a right or wrong way to react when someone we love is grieving, but there are some things that may help support them. Sometimes just being with them will be just enough. If you have lost a person close to you, there are many ways that you can honor their memory. It is important to remember the loved one in your own way, which means being comfortable with what feels suitable for you.

People grieve in different ways, but the experience is universal. Grief is a harrowing experience, but it is also part of the natural healing process. There are many things people can do to help ease the pain of grief, and remember that grieving takes time. There are many different ways to deal with grief, and no one way is suitable for everyone. Maybe your pain will never pass, but you will learn to live with it in time.

Made in the USA
Monee, IL
19 September 2023

42980346R00033